Benefits of Artificial Intelligence

CHRISTA KELLY

childsworld.com

Published by The Child's World®
800-599-READ • www.childsworld.com

Photography Credits
Photographs ©: DC Studio/Shutterstock Images, cover, 1; Shutterstock Images, 5, 9, 10, 15 (top), 15 (bottom), 16, 19, 20; IM Imagery/Shutterstock Images, 7; NASA Images/Shutterstock Images, 13; Design elements from Tatiana Shepeleva/Shutterstock Images and Shutterstock Images

ISBN Information
9781503893788 (Reinforced Library Binding)
9781503894600 (Portable Document Format)
9781503895423 (Online Multi-user eBook)
9781503896246 (Electronic Publication)

LCCN 2024941392

Printed in the United States of America

ABOUT THE AUTHOR

Christa Kelly is an author and editor from Minnesota. She lives with her wife, Clare, and their two cats, Casey and Honey Cheddar.

CONTENTS

CHAPTER ONE

HELPING IN A HURRICANE

Scientists watch their **radar**. They are tracking the weather over a small town by the ocean. A big hurricane is about to hit. But most of the people in town have already left. The scientists' computers had predicted the storm. The computers helped the scientists **forecast** when and where the hurricane would land. The scientists were able to warn the people in the town.

The hurricane hits. The powerful storm rips trees out of the ground. It destroys buildings. After it passes, rescuers launch a flying robot called a drone. The drone soars over the town. It takes pictures of the city. It sees which buildings were damaged the most. This information helps the rescuers decide who needs help first.

Rescuers launch more drones over the city. These drones scan for survivors. One drone spots a small child. It alerts a rescue team. The team brings the child to safety.

Some drones use artificial intelligence to pilot themselves.

Within a few hours, dozens of people have been rescued. Some are hurt. But the damage could have been worse without the scientists and rescue teams. They saved many lives. And they could not have done it without artificial intelligence (AI).

The scientists' computers and drones all use AI. AI is an area of computer science. It focuses on using computers to do complicated tasks. These tasks include writing, making decisions, and **analyzing** large amounts of **data**. Until recently, only humans could do many of these tasks.

Some machines use AI to learn. These machines get better at their tasks over time. Some are eventually able to do their jobs better than humans.

AI has many benefits. It can save people time by doing repetitive work. It often makes fewer errors than humans. It can work faster than people. It can handle huge amounts of data. And unlike human workers, AI does not need to rest or take breaks.

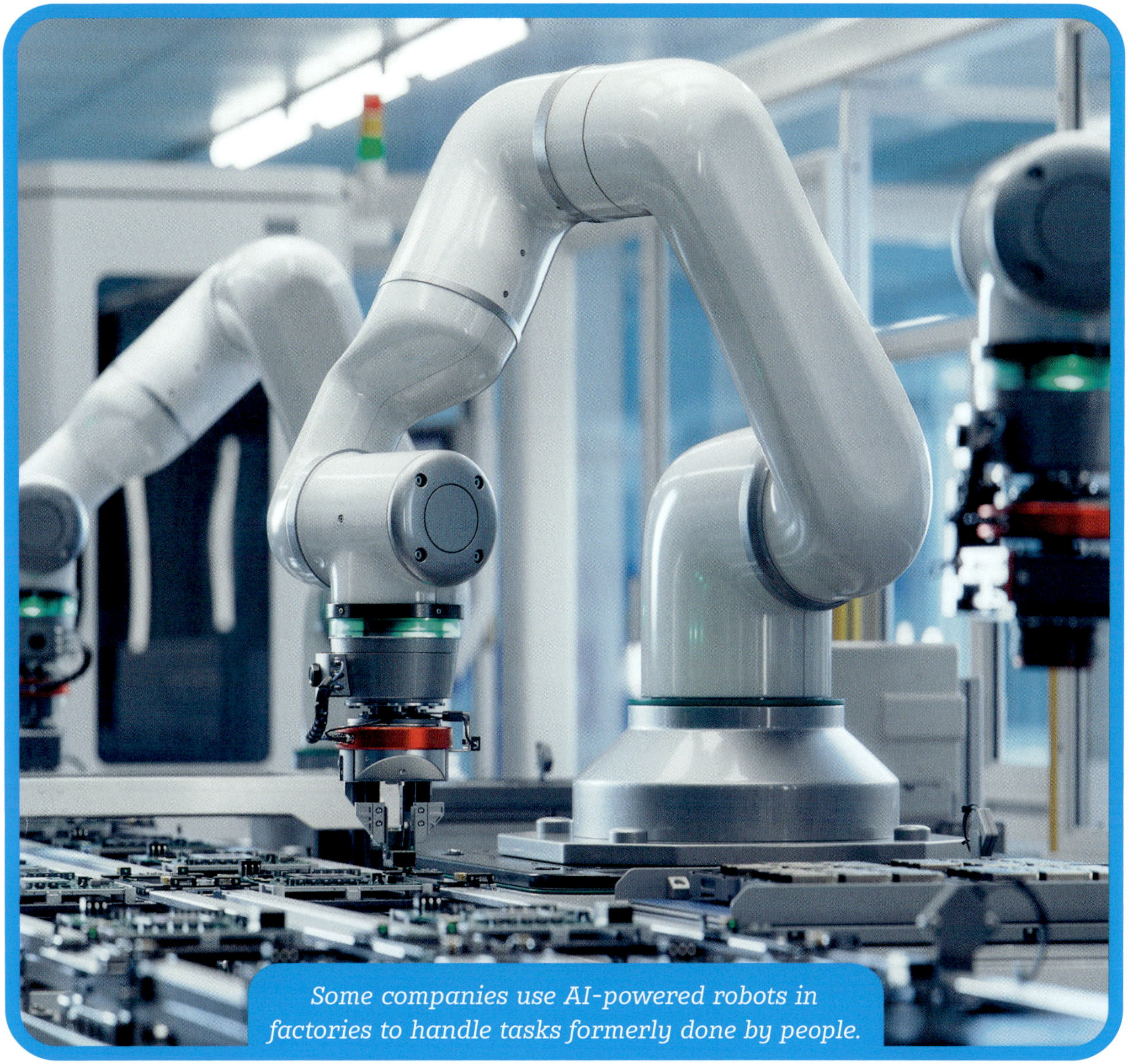

Some companies use AI-powered robots in factories to handle tasks formerly done by people.

People use AI in many ways. Doctors use AI to help patients. Scientists use AI to predict natural disasters. And some companies are even teaching AI to drive cars. As technology develops, scientists will find new ways for AI to help the world.

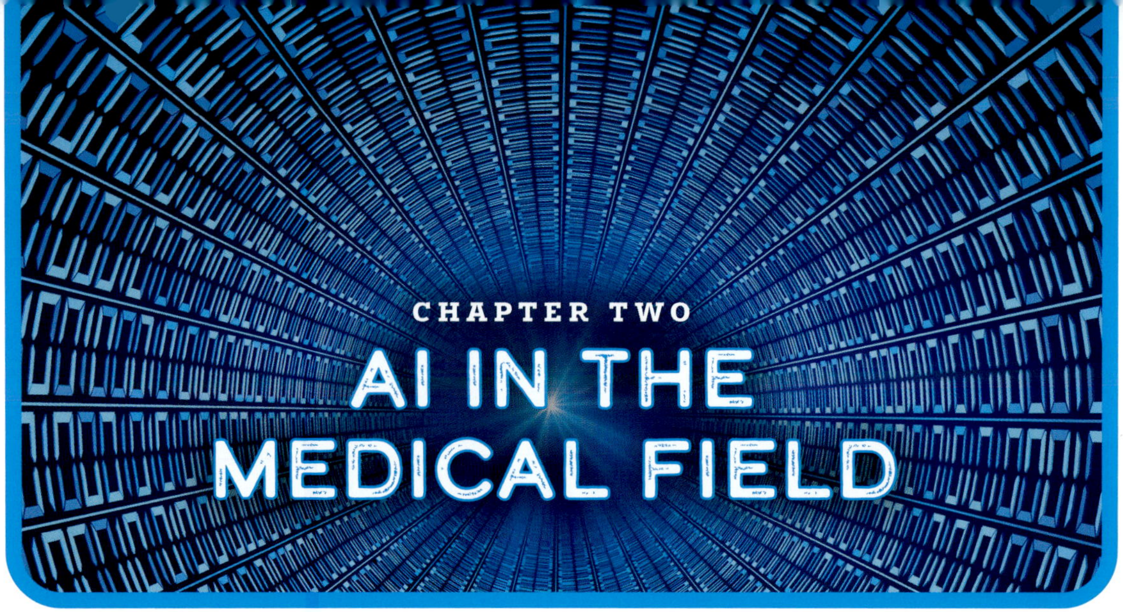

CHAPTER TWO

AI IN THE MEDICAL FIELD

Health care workers have many responsibilities. Nurses talk to patients and take notes. Researchers invent new medicines. Doctors **diagnose** illnesses. AI can help with many of these tasks.

Generative AI is one kind of AI being used in health care. This type of AI can generate, or create, new content. This content includes text, images, and videos. Generative AI can be used to make chatbots. These are computer programs that can hold humanlike conversations. Chatbots can help patients with basic tasks, such as scheduling appointments and handling billing. In 2023, a medical company revealed that 96 percent of patients who interacted with the company's medical chatbot said they had a positive experience.

Chatbots have uses beyond the health care field. People can use chatbots to help them answer questions or write.

Doctors can use generative AI to take notes. Doctors record their conversations with patients. Generative AI analyzes the recordings and collects the important information. Then it turns the audio recordings into text for the doctor to read. This allows doctors to spend more time on other tasks.

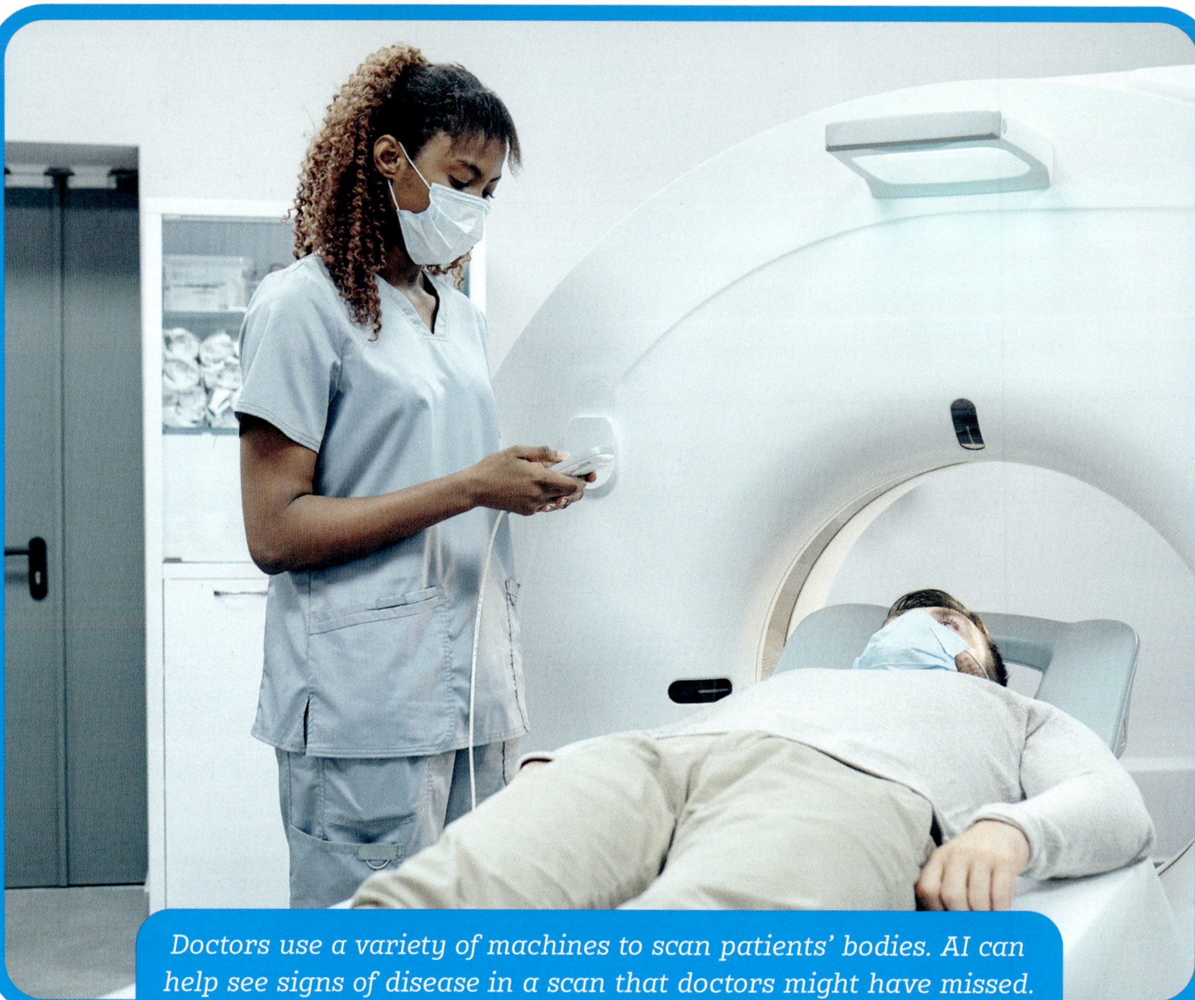

Doctors use a variety of machines to scan patients' bodies. AI can help see signs of disease in a scan that doctors might have missed.

Other types of AI can be used to diagnose patients. Some doctors are using AI to diagnose cancer. They show scans of tumors to AI programs. Tumors are abnormal growths in a person's body that can sometimes be cancerous. The programs also look at healthy scans. These scans help the AI learn how to recognize the difference between healthy tissue and unhealthy tissue.

The AI is then able to spot tumors on its own. A 2020 study found that an AI program was better at detecting lung cancer than human professionals.

AI can even help invent new medicines. Many medicines contain **proteins**. Different proteins do different things in the body. Some proteins fight diseases. Others can save people from snake bites. But coming up with a new protein to use as medicine is complicated. The process can take years of work and billions of dollars. However, AI can do this work in just months. Using generative AI, scientists are able to create new proteins. The AI designs the proteins and the scientists produce them. This can save time, money, and lives.

WORKING WITH AI

AI is unlikely to completely replace human workers. Instead, people are learning to work alongside AI. Doctors who diagnose cancer still look at scans. They use AI to make sure they do not miss anything. Researchers who make new medicines use AI to speed up their work, but they still carefully design and control experiments.

CHAPTER THREE

AI TO THE RESCUE

Natural disasters are dangerous events caused by environmental factors. These events include hurricanes and earthquakes. Natural disasters kill thousands of people every year. But people are using AI to reduce the damage from these events.

Natural disasters are difficult for scientists to predict. Even with modern technology, it is hard to know when and where natural disasters will strike. Without advance warning, people do not know to leave an area or take cover before a disaster hits. This can lead to injuries and deaths.

AI can help scientists track the path of a hurricane.

AI can help improve natural disaster predictions. Scientists give AI huge amounts of data about past disasters. The AI finds patterns in the data. It learns how to spot signs that a disaster might occur. It makes scientists' predictions more accurate. It also analyzes data more quickly than humans can. This allows it to warn people earlier. Early warnings allow people to prepare before a disaster strikes. This saves lives.

AI can also save lives after a natural disaster strikes. In 2023, a massive earthquake hit Turkey. Thousands of people were trapped under rubble. Rescuers had to decide who to help first. They turned to an AI program called xView2 for help. This program analyzes **satellite images** of areas affected by natural disasters. It looks at the damage done to buildings. It highlights the buildings hit hardest in red. Rescuers then know to go to these buildings first. It used to take rescuers weeks to determine which areas needed help the most. But xView2 can complete the process in just hours. It is also very accurate. The program is good at figuring out how bad the damage is.

WHAT DOES XVIEW2 SEE?

Real Photo

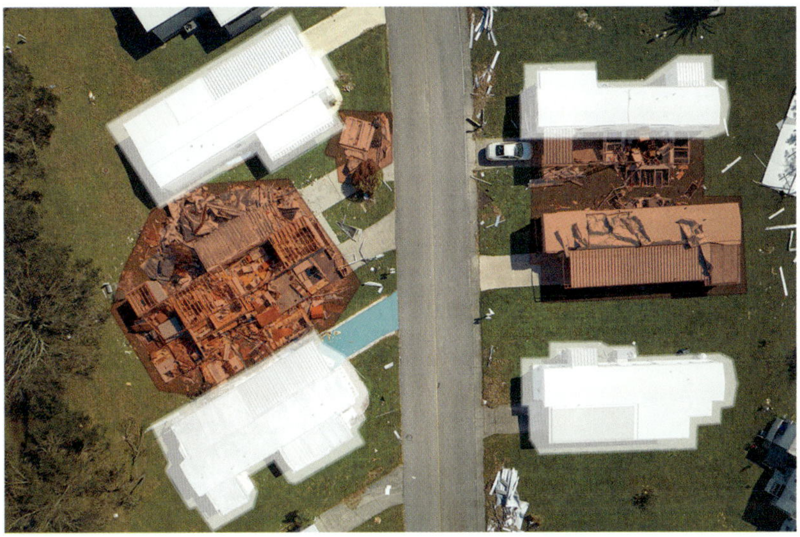

What xView2 Sees

xView2 uses the color red to draw attention to damaged buildings. It uses white to mark areas that are not damaged.

Two members of a sea rescue team perform a practice rescue.

In Turkey, xView2 helped volunteers quickly organize rescue missions. It also helped rescuers locate damaged areas. In the end, more than 8,000 people were rescued from collapsed buildings.

As AI technology improves, scientists hope it can help with disasters in other ways, too. The US Coast Guard partnered with an AI company to improve rescue missions. The company began developing technology that can find people who are lost at sea. The technology uses sensors that are more reliable than human eyesight. Using this technology could allow search-and-rescue teams to find people at night or in fog. This could save many lives.

CHAPTER FOUR

TRAVELING WITH AI

AI is completely changing transportation. Many new cars use AI in a number of safety features. For example, some cars have cameras that check the area around the car. AI can look at the images recorded by the cameras to tell if people are in them. That way, the car can warn the driver to be safe around the people. This can help reduce accidents.

AI can also prevent speeding. Some newer cars are built with intelligent speed assistance (ISA). This technology uses AI-powered cameras that read speed limit signs. It can also use map data to determine the speed limit in a given area. Some ISA systems alert drivers when they are going over the speed limit. Others can stop the vehicle from speeding at all. Studies have found that these systems can reduce speeding. Researchers think that ISA systems could reduce road deaths.

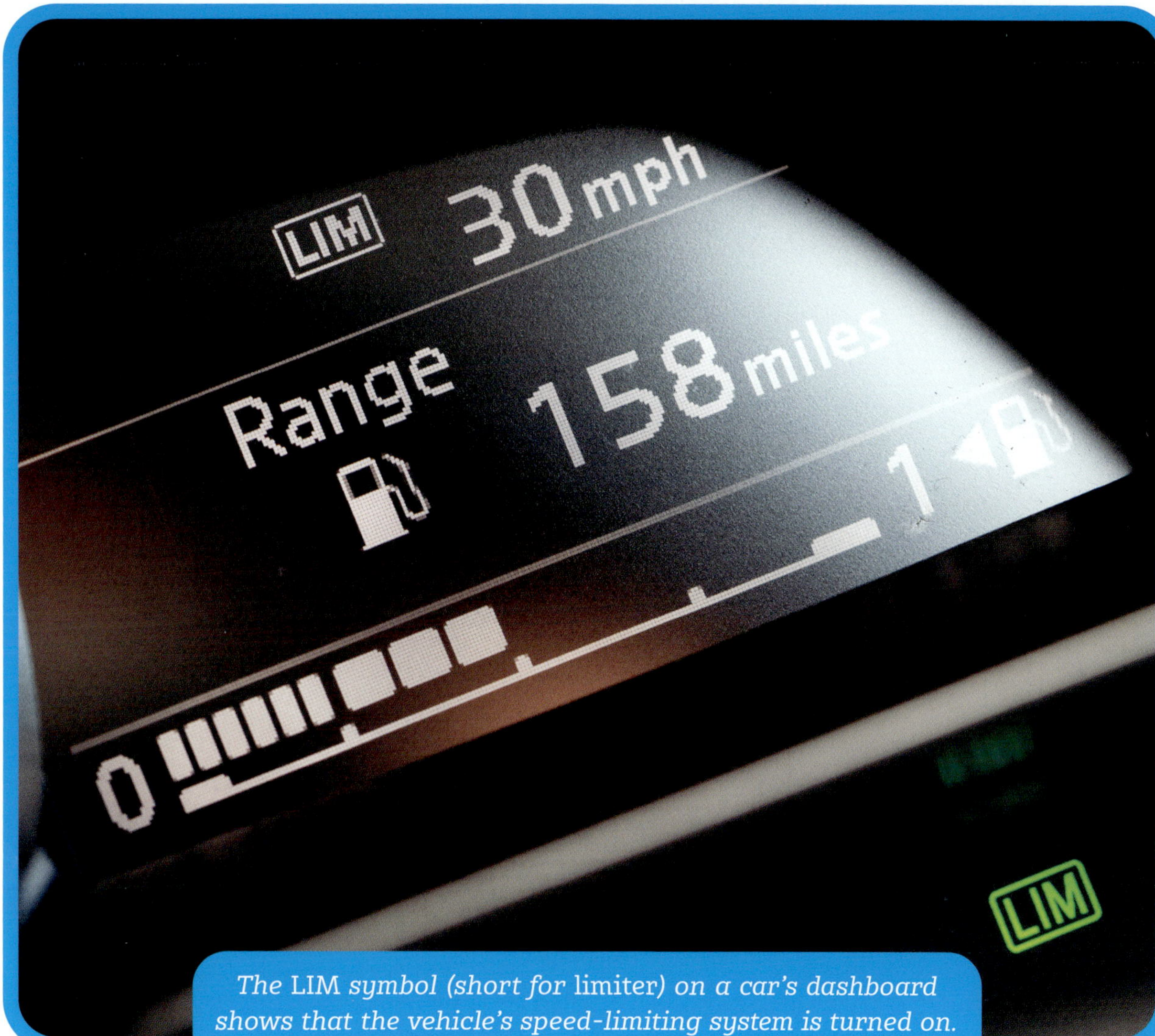

The LIM symbol (short for limiter) on a car's dashboard shows that the vehicle's speed-limiting system is turned on.

Some companies are even developing self-driving cars. These cars use AI to allow passengers to relax while the car drives for them. The AI controls the car's speed and steering. It can make safe decisions, such as stopping when a person crosses the road ahead. And the AI can learn from its experiences while driving.

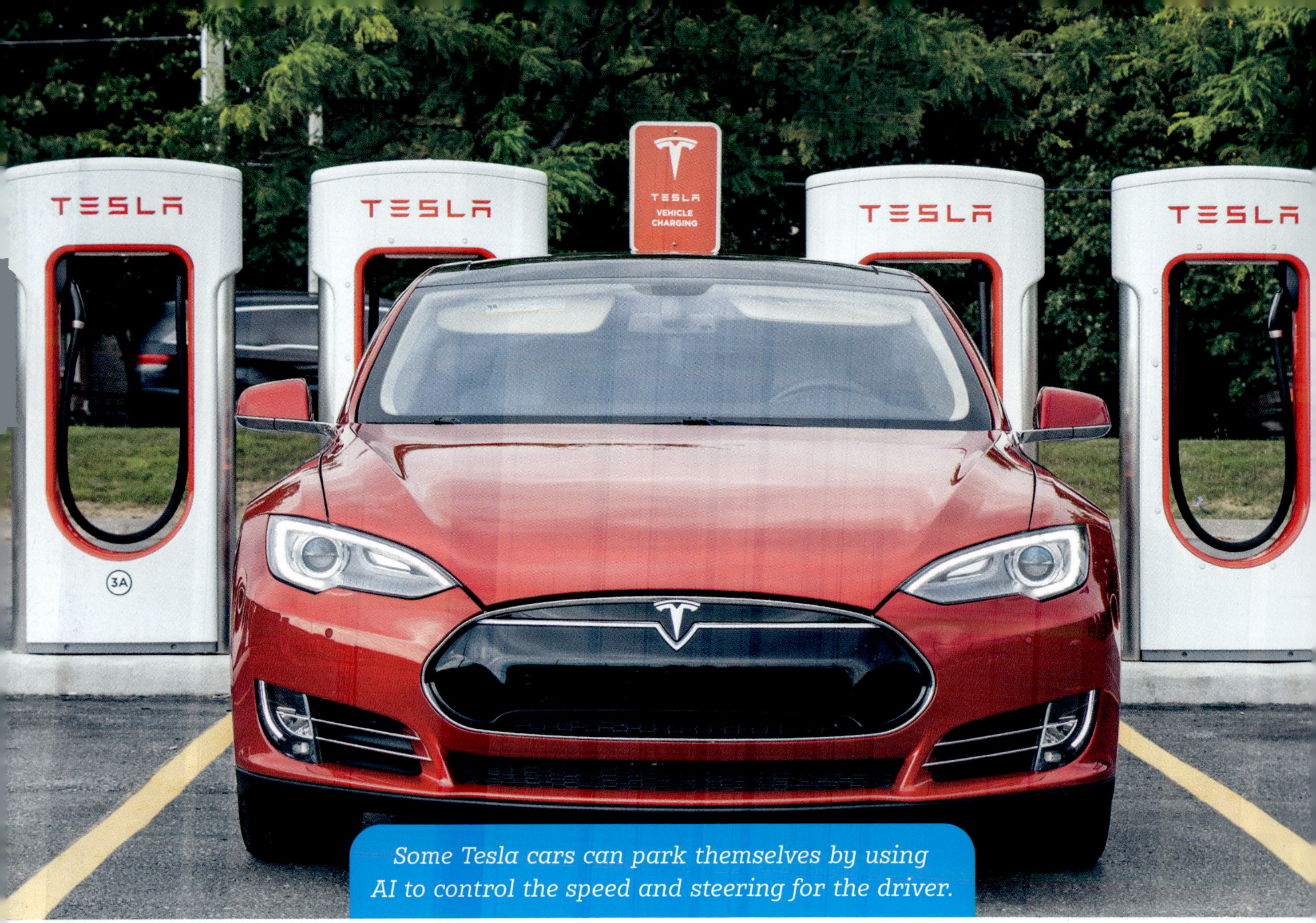

Some Tesla cars can park themselves by using AI to control the speed and steering for the driver.

The company Motional made a self-driving car that works like a taxi. It made more than 100,000 trips without causing one at-fault accident. Waymo is a similar company. Driverless Waymo cars have driven more than 7 million miles (11 million km). The cars are 85 percent less likely than human-driven cars to be involved in a crash resulting in injury. This means that self-driving cars could be safer than human-driven cars.

Other companies are making self-driving technology directly available to buyers. The car manufacturer Tesla makes cars that can steer, navigate routes, and manage speed **autonomously**. However, these cars must be supervised by drivers. Researchers say that drivers are still years away from owning their own fully self-driving cars.

AI helps people in many different ways. But researchers are pushing it to do even more. As AI technology improves, people will find new benefits of this incredible technology.

AI IN MANUFACTURING

Some manufacturers use AI to make vehicles. BMW is one such company. Robots help assemble vehicles. Then, AI programs use cameras to check that vehicles were put together correctly. If the AI finds an error, it tells the robots how to fix it. This makes vehicle assembly more **efficient**. It also costs less than using human workers.

GLOSSARY

analyzing (AN-uh-lye-zing) When people or computers are analyzing something, they are closely examining it. Analyzing large amounts of information takes less time for AI than it does for humans.

autonomously (ot-ON-uh-muss-lee) Technology that works autonomously does tasks on its own without human assistance. Self-driving cars can brake and change lanes autonomously.

data (DAY-tuh) Data is information collected for a purpose. AI programs can learn from data by analyzing it.

diagnose (dye-ig-NOHSS) To diagnose a medical condition is to determine what kind of condition it is. AI can help doctors diagnose cancer.

efficient (ih-FIH-shunt) Something is efficient if it works without being wasteful. Some car companies use AI to make producing cars more efficient.

forecast (FOR-kast) When scientists forecast something, they predict when and where it will happen. AI helps scientists forecast natural disasters.

proteins (PRO-teens) Proteins are complex substances that do important tasks to keep people healthy. Proteins fight bacteria, build muscles, and help people grow.

radar (RAY-dar) Radar is a tool that uses radio waves to detect objects. Scientists can use radar to see the locations of storms.

satellite images (SA-tuh-lyte IH-muh-jiz) Satellite images are photos of Earth taken by machines in space called satellites. AI can use satellite images to track storms.

FAST FACTS

- Artificial intelligence (AI) is an area of computer science that focuses on making computers do tasks that normally require human intelligence.
- Generative AI is used in health care to communicate with patients. It can also be used to help doctors take notes. Doctors can use AI programs to help them detect cancer. AI can also help create new medicines.
- AI can predict natural disasters such as hurricanes and earthquakes. This gives people time to prepare before conditions become dangerous. After a natural disaster strikes, rescuers can use AI to determine which areas need help first.
- AI safety features are included in many vehicles. These systems help drivers make safe driving decisions, such as avoiding obstacles and reducing speed.
- Some companies have developed self-driving cars to serve as taxis.

ONE STRIDE FURTHER

- Would you be comfortable talking to an AI chatbot about medical issues? Why or why not?
- What are some additional ways artificial intelligence could benefit people?
- Why might some people be worried about the rise of AI-powered self-driving cars?

FIND OUT MORE

IN THE LIBRARY

Kulz, George Anthony. *What Is Artificial Intelligence?* Parker, CO: The Child's World, 2025.

Rathburn, Betsy. *Self-Driving Cars*. Minneapolis, MN: Bellwether, 2021.

Williams, Haley. *Artificial Intelligence in Everyday Life*. Parker, CO: The Child's World, 2025.

ON THE WEB

Visit our website for links about the benefits of artificial intelligence:
childsworld.com/links

Note to Parents, Caregivers, Teachers, and Librarians: We routinely verify our web links to make sure they are safe and active sites. So encourage your readers to check them out!

INDEX